Verses & Things

No part of this publication may be reproduced or transmitted in any form by any means, electronic or mechanical, including photocopying and recording, or by any information storage and retrieval system, except as may be expressly permitted in writing by the author.

Dedicated to:

My daughter, Madison, who I love and cherish with all my heart.

My Mom, Joyce, who taught me to read at an early age.

Many thanks to:

Jordyn L. Willis (IG- @meugata), who provided the cover art;

Ron Akines (IG- @misterakines), who provided the illustrations on pages 27, 44, 65, 68, & 72; and

Thaddaeus Watson, who made sure my Spanish was on point.

UMM... HI.

Thank you for being willing to read my very first book.

I had my reservations when it was suggested to me that I write a book of poetry. Would people like it? Why would anybody really be interested in *my* poetry? Is what I have written *really* worth reading? These and many more questions had arisen. Ultimately, I came to the conclusion that I do not care if some do not like it- there are some who will (thanks Mom), some who are interested, some who will find it worth reading. At the very least, I published my first book!!! That is one item off of my list of things to do before I die.

Poetry is many things to many people. It is a look inside hearts and minds; a cry for social and/or political change; a cry for help; an apology; a descent into darkness, and a resurrection to light; a lamentation of broken hearts, and the exultation of newfound love. Poetry is a means to say things that otherwise cannot be expressed, or should not. It is an escape from, or an awakening to, one's reality. Whatever its meaning, poetry moves; and those moved write poetry.

My first poem came as a result of a disappointment that saddened me (thanks D.M.S.). After that very first poem, I realized that I had somewhat of a talent. And over the years, I've written poems mostly of love and its various facets- lust, desire, longing, attraction, rejection, loss, etc., etc. It was a humbling experience preparing this book, because I am opening myself up in a way that I am not familiar or comfortable with. Sharing my innermost thoughts and feelings, past or present, is an idea that is foreign. But I am glad that I have faced whatever fears I had and have come this far.

I hope readers enjoy what I have written.

Okay, enough of the 'cheese'. Let's go…

TABLE OF CONTENTS

TABLE OF CONTENTS (cont'd)

Your Favorite Things

Your favorite song, your favorite book,
your favorite show at which to look;
Your favorite scarf, your favorite gloves,
I want to be your favorite love.

Your favorite dress, your favorite jeans,
I wanna know your favorite things.
Your favorite poem, your favorite verse,
let me know it, I'll rehearse.

Your favorite planet, favorite star,
I'll bring it to you, near or far.
Your favorite color, favorite hue,
the favorite things you like to do.

Your favorite spot I long to kiss;
let mine be your favorite lips.
The favorite hand you love to hold,
may it be mine as we grow old.

I want to know what brings you pleasure,
so I may be all that you treasure.
Your favorite love, may it be me.
May I be your favorite eternally.

... AND I EXPLODE

Every time I think about you my heartbeat quickens

My blood reaches its boiling point

My temperature escalates...

...And I explode.

Every ounce of my soul longs to have you near

Longs to feel your nakedness next to mine

All my love for you rises,

and reaches out to you

To feel you surround it with a passion ungoverned

A passion wet with desire.

And from the very second I feel you touch me

The moment I feel your passion engulf my love

My heartbeat quickens

My blood boils...

...And I explode

ANGIE

she is as black as the night is dark, and as

luminescent as the stars that shine in the

midnight sky.

Her beauty shines brighter than diamonds

yet is contained by her humility.

She has a smile that melts glaciers, and a

touch that can calm a storm.

I am gifted to have her as a friend, but

I'd be blessed if I could only have

her heart.

I have yet to taste the ever sweet passion

that flows within her soft

supple breasts.

To have her as my queen, I'd sacrifice

wealth beyond wealth.

For truly she is more than a work of art.

Do I

Do I owe you an apology for falling in love with you?

Need I explain why I let myself fall for you?

Does my current life situation

Mean, from my feelings, I must take a vacation?

True, I've been abandoned, left to my devices,

But refusing to give vent to all my many vices.

Thankfully, to me you've been gifted

And my pain of heart's been finally lifted.

Every One of Your freckles

Every one of your freckles shines like the stars at night,

Making your face as astounding as the evening sky.

And, may I say, lady, you're a breathtaking sight.

There's no doubt you're a marvelous sight.

Every one of your curves I have traced with my eyes,

Caressing your body, but not using my hands.

Front to back, top to bottom, and side to side.

And from you, the truth I won't hide.

Your flesh so soft, like that of a feather's touch;

I long to be with you skin-to-skin.

It should be obvious to you that I desire you much

Yes, lady, I want you so much.

Untitled #1

I wanted so much to be your friend,

Content with only that.

I never thought about loving you,

Never thought about wanting you,

Never thought about wanting to be

More than just your friend.

overextended

I'm sorry.

I have overextended my reach,

Daring to exceed my boundaries,

Daring to escape the "zone".

I'm sorry.

For letting myself have feelings

For you, but can you really blame me?

You are quite a true beauty. But...

Our friendship

Is not enough for one such as I.

I want you for myself, for always,

As long as Jehovah lives.

After Bliss

If I want you so badly now,

Wait til we share our first kiss.

And after that will you bear

My desire for you after bliss?

LIKE WATER

Like water, my love, you are everywhere.

My mind, my heart, and even in my pores.

I breathe you, 'cause you're in my lungs;

I bleed you, 'cause you're in my veins;

I dream you, 'cause you own my thoughts.

And like an addict, of your love I crave more.

Picture Us

Picture me, your husband,
rushing home from work
to get a taste of your sweet lovin'.

Then, our son, the second,
Drivin' you so crazy.
,cause that's what boys do, I reckon.

Then our daughter, Brooke-
In the kitchen with you
To learn how, like you, to cook.

Picture us, together
The two of us as one,
Unitedly Loving each other forever.

MAKE NO MISTAKE

Do not make the mistake
of thinking that I will forget.
Don't believe that I will
ignore what I feel about you.

Loving you's my choice to make;
For this love I have no regrets.
Don't think that my love will chill
If I'm separated from you.

Don't think that they'll go away,
The emotions I have, so strong.
On this matter I'm dead set,
Concentrated, focused, on you.

Love's for e'er, I need to say.
To let go, to me'd be so wrong.
My love I'll ne'er forget,
'cause, woman, I truly love you.

That Someone Is You

I lost sleep over someone I do not wake up to.
That someone is you.

Those minutes tossing and turning are well worth the loss,
for someone like you.

I'll lose sleep over someone I do not wake up to.
That someone is you.

I cry at night over one I do not wake up to,
And that one is you.

I dream every night of one I do not wake up to.
Again, she is you.

I pray every night "Jah give me one to wake up to".
I'm praying for you.

I do all of the foolish things that I do, 'cause I
love someone. that's you.

The Many Years Between Us

The many years between us is nothing but a number,

The years we have ahead are the only ones that matter.

The love shared between us is nothing on which to slumber

With forever up ahead love will only grow fatter.

You & I both share a secret no one else dares to know;

It's in your eyes & in my smile, & writ large on my sleeve.

For my part, dear, I can't help it, my love for you must show.

And you, I hope, feel the same as this web of love we weave.

The joy i feel when I'm with you grows greater every day.

To hear your voice, & to see your smile brings me such great

joy.

I long for when you're mine, & with your body I can play.

For now I'll wait impatiently, just like a little boy.

I love you, woman. This you know- I love you to no end.

I long to be your husband, lover- more than just your friend.

There's This One

There's this one that moves me
More so by her character
Than by her looks.

Please, Don't misunderstand me,
She is a "dime piece",
A head turner.

But she's far, far more than that.
She's modest, humble,
A lover of God.

She has dreams, ambitions, focus
She knows what she wants
And she will get it.

She's a joy to be around, to have around
She knows have to have fun
And when to be serious.

I can trust her with my feelings ,
Confide my vulnerabilities-
I trust her with my heart's heart.

There's this one I love more than I should.
She's stolen my thoughts,
And she's all I dreamed of.

WHY??

Your face,

Your shape,

Your hair,

Your freckles,

Your smile,

Your style,

Your skin,

Your arms,

Your hands,

Your legs,

Your lips,

Your cute little feet,

Your attitude,

Your modesty,

Your coolness,

Your inner beauty,

Your you.

If you ever wonder why, this is just the tip of the tip of the iceberg.

When I was thirteen, and she was twelve, we met at her cousin's birthday party. She sat at one end of her aunt's sofa, and immediately upon my entering the room caught my eyes, and my heart. I fell. Hard. Being the extremely shy kid that I was, I never had the courage to tell her directly how and what I felt. This, the fear of being rejected by *her*, was my problem. I grew callous to rejection by others; but from her I did not think I would be able to deal with it. Years went by and yet I never voiced how I felt, to her.

Throughout the years we grew to be friends, but my heart craved more; eventually to be disappointed. There were others I tried to fill the void with, but they never compared or measured up to her. There were some I have loved, but she was, not the "one that got away"- as that implies that her love and her heart were once mine to treausre, but the one I was doomed to love unrequitedly.

I've been hurt before, but the pain that still cuts, even three decades later, is the pain of having to hear the woman you desperately love tell you she's carrying someone else's child. Talk about emotional Armageddon! That, for me, was life changing. For some reason it still hurts.

Our paths have crossed over the years, and every time those feelings, those memories, flood my heart and mind. Even when she calls my name, it stops me dead in my tracks and chills my spine.

The last time I saw her I held her tightly and finally told her that I love her. Not loved, but love. I have never stopped. Even though we may never be together (a brother can dream, though), those feelings will continue to haunt me. And yet, like a lovesick fool, I will continue to hope…

These ten are for and about and because of her.

Enjoy.

The voice of a woman

The voice of a woman

Is sensual, enticing, welcoming, inviting

The voice of a woman

Is all I need to hear

To escape from all my fear

So let's get one thing clear,

Nothing eases pain like…

the voice of a woman.

For T.

A love once lost

A love once lost, but now regained
This kind of love has caused me pain
This kind of love is hard to find
I once thought. I once opined

Recaptured love that blows my mind.
What I thought I lost just took some time.
This kind of love is hard to find.
I can't believe It's now you & me.

This love is true,
And all for you.
This love is mine.
And for all time
I'll be loving you
I'll be loving you

I had to wait for Jah to hear
& for me to see precious love so near.
Eternal love; And now it's mine
You & me... Eternally.

For T.

Untitled #10

In 1990 the call came, and I answered;

Not for duty or country or honor or glory.

I did not cower, I did not hide, I did not run away.

I served with my unit, my brothers in blood,

So that on a battlefield would begin the story

Of one who faced his greatest threat-

Love denied, not another. Of one who

Faced fire and fury and lead and steel

Only to "die" of a broken heart. No,

Ne'er at the hands or the blade of another,

But by news that would pierce his heart

Months before the orders came. And

And many years later, that Marine's heart

Has yet to heal.

For T.

Like the Wind In My Hands...

Time and tears have told me that she's like the wind in my hands

Trying to possess her is like trying to count earth's grains of sand;

Every blade of grass, every tree that stands, every drop that falls,

Every snowflake, every star, every brick in every wall

Time will not allow me to repeat our only kiss

The years will not return to the moment that I've missed.

I was but a boy in love, now a man with a tormented soul

To have to feel her soft, warm lips every day till I grow old.

To always wonder how life would be with her at my side,

To always think, "If only I could cross this very great divide

Of time, of age, of passing years, of days come and past.

If only I could say something to make that one kiss last."

My feelings have not differed, from boyhood to a man

But as time and tears have shown me, she's like the wind in my hands.

For T.

Yesterday's Epiphany

Yesterday I realized there IS that one person who embeds themselves so deeply into your heart, that you cannot let that one go.

Yesterday I was reminded of WHO true love is, what it felt like, and how enduring it is; I was reminded about how incomparable REAL love is.

Yesterday I realized that what I thought I knew about love-romantic love, was nothing compared to:
the way my heart stopped when I saw her smile,
the way I freeze in my tracks when I hear her voice,
how she has not aged a day since I first met her.

Yesterday my mind was blown with the understanding of what real love is, and how it should feel.

For T.

holding on to memories

I keep holding on to memories of a love that never came to be, of a love that was never meant for me, of a love I was never meant to see.

And each time I try to let her go my heart cries out and tells me NO. My heart doesn't wanna let her go. No, I don't wanna let her go.

Effortlessly, my heart she's won. In the world of 9 billion, she's the one. I'd drop it all, yes, to her I'd run. 'Cause my love for her burns like the sun.

So, I'll keep holding on to the memory of a love I was never meant to see, of a love that never came to be, of the love that was NEVER meant for me.

But I'll keep hoping that the day will come
when I am hers and we'll be one;
when I am hers and I''ll get to see
the reality of what was made for me.

For T.

Untitled #11

No matter where I go, what I do, there's always one thought that stays with me.

>
> And it's that one thought that haunts perpetually my mind, my heart, my soul.

Even though I've had many others, and many others have had me,

>
> NO ONE has touched me, moved me, no one has plagued me as much as she.

Even on the other side of the world she was with me, taunting me

>
> In my dreams at night, and during the day, she's there to tease me.

My dream, my desire, my goal is still to have her, hold her, touch her,

>
> But that dream will yet remain a dream.

For T.

I WISH I COULD...

I wish I could tell you
what goes on in my mind everytime I see you...
                              but I can't.

I wish I could share with you
all the things I feel when I think about you...
                              but I can't

I wish my lips would say
what my heart wants you to know...
                              but they can't

I wish I could take you
and hold you in my arms for a lifetime...
                              if only you'd let me.

I wish I knew what I feel for you...
but, no matter how much I try,
                              I can't.

I wish I could tell you
how much, how very much, I love you...

                              but I can't...

For T.

For A Thousand Years

I have loved you for a thousand years,

and, if I had to, I'd love you a thousand times more.

A thousand times I've dreamed of you,

and I'll dream of you a thousand times more.

I've held you close a thousand times;

      felt the warmth of your love;

      embraced the reality of our dreams;

      touched the heavens while looking in your eyes;

and I'll do it all a thousand times over.

A thousand times I died for you,

and, for you, I'd die a thousand times more.

For T.

That elusive thing

Ages upon ages I've sought
That elusive thing.

Hard were the lessons she taught,
That elusive thing.

Wind in my hand she's become
So elusive a thing

Peace in my heart's come undone
By that elusive thing

E're by loneliness I'm taunted
With that elusive thing

Perpetually my soul is haunted
By that elusive thing

Forever I'm damned to seek
For that which makes me weak
And for that with pain it brings,
For love's the elusive thing.

For T.

IT'S ME

In case you're wondering who it was that
    erased away your pain, your hurt

who picked you up when you had fallen,
    who wiped from you this world's dirt

who stood beside you in times of trouble and
    who walked with you through your fears

who lent his shoulder and dried your eyes
    who also shared your tears

if you need to know the man that held you
    in his arms, so close, so tight

who kept you safe from all the badness,
    all the monsters in the night

if you're wondering who this one is, my love,
    open your heart, your eyes, and see

the one always there for you, loves you
    and if you're wondering... it's me.

THEN SHALL I

Let thine own lips say, "Nay, I love thee not",

Else shall I revere thee as mine own.

My love doth have no bounds, 'tis limited by a word from thee.

Ne'er again shall my love be known amongst men

If thy lips spake thy heart's passions.

For if thy heart doth love me not,

Then truly I shall be most bereaved 'mong men.

I shall revile my own soul, if thy love for me is naught.

Let thine own lips say, "Nay, I love thee not",

Then shall I die in tears.

Let thine own lips say, "Henceforth, I am yours",

Else shall I be lost evermore.

My love doth have no patience, 'tis awaiting but a word.

Ne'er again shall my passion be besmirched 'mong men,

For thy lips hath committed to me thy love.

For truly I shall be most praised amongst men.

I shall bubble over with joy, for thy love for me is true.

Let thine own lips say, "Henceforth, I am yours",

Then shall I live anew.

Let thine own lips answer me with but a word.

LOVE UNDISCOVERED

Whatever secrets there are for us to share,
will remain forever uncovered.

Whatever passions, too, between me and you,
will be a treasure left undiscovered.

The thunderous roar of my heart shall never be heard.
And all the visions I have of you shall henceforth be blurred.

Hands, not to hold!
Lips, ne'er to kiss!

I reach out to touch you,
and I am embracing a mere mist.

The thoughts that we share, when we look at each other,
shall forever be concealed.

And the love that we feel, although brightly it shines,
is ne'er to be revealed!

Untitled #2

No, you are not the most beautiful woman in *the* world.

But that is not who I want.

I want the woman who makes *my* world more beautiful.

No, no eres la mujer más bella *del* mundo.

Pero eso no es lo que quiero.

Quiero a la mujer que hace *mi* mundo más hermoso.

Beauty From Of Old

The sun will cast its golden shadow
   over all the earth.
And a flame can shake and wiggle and dance
   in the comfort of a hearth.

The moon, the sentinel of the night,
   will guard the midnight sky.
And the stars, legions of voiceless wonder,
   command attention from the eye.

But you my darling like all these,
   possess lovliness from of old.
And for such beauty, as in the past,
   stories have been told.

For the power of the beauty
   that you are and that you hold
has seized all vital parts of me-
My mind,
My heart,
My soul.

ODE TO HER

There are no words in all the human
languages that could describe your beauty,

no scale on which to measure,

no gem nor precious stone or metal could
even compare.

your beauty is more calming than a
symphony of birds & more soothing than
the sound of the sea,

more wondrous than a sunset, and more
exquisite than pearls,

when the sun shines upon you the clouds
bow down, the wind sings a song, and the
mountains applaud.

to your beauty the moon makes his toast
and the stars stand silently amazed.

you are a dream's fulfillment, a prayer's
answer, and the culmination of all the
beauty that has ever been created, born,
or imagined,

you are the gold at the end of my rainbow,
the silver lining of my cloud.

men, even I marvel at your beauty,
for it is truly a breathtaking sight.

if only you could behold your own beauty
through my eyes.

Untitled #3

JUST A KISS FROM YOU WILL COOL ME...

JUST A TOUCH FROM YOU WILL SAVE ME ...

JUST A LOOK FROM YOU WILL PIERCE ME...

JUST A MOMENT WITH YOU...

Give me a moment to be
Inside of you, eternally.
Never will I be sated.
Give me just a moment and I
Evermore will you satisfy.
Reward me with love unstated.

Me, Without You?

Can there be no ocean without a beach;

No sun without a moon?

What good feelings if kept within,

A clock when there's no time?

Can there be no dreams unless one sleeps;

A song sans melody?

What purpose vict'ry without a win;

Diamonds- with no shine?

Why have the means & not share in giving,

speak words if none are true?

What is the meaning of my living

If it must be done without you?

Untitled #4

Tell me one good tale of falling in Love

I'll tell you ten tales of losing it.

Show me the right way of being in love

And I'll be the fool not choosing it

'Cause I'll never know love the way you know love.

I'm more familiar with the pain of heart.

I'll never know love the way you know love.

So there's no need for me to even start.

Untitled #5

It's been years.

There've been tears.

We've had to fight our way through with each other

And our fears.

Yes, i cried.

And i tried.

I love you now, forever, and always

I never lied.

I Wish I Could Cry

I wish I could cry, but the tears won't flow.

Just one tear, and I pray I'll feel better.

Pain, emotional pain, the kind that rips one in half,

        the kind that make one wish for death,

        the kind of pain that's never-ending.

    Alone again...

        ... as usual.

It hurts. Loving without being loved,

    Caring, without being cared about,

    Reaching out, only to grasp

Emptiness, for she is no longer there to fulfill me...

Darkness, because her smile will no longer brighten my day...

Coldness, for I will no longer feel her warm embrace.

    I wish we could start over again, maybe things will be

different,

        maybe we could right what was wrong.

    I wish we were together again.

    I wish...

        ... I wish I could cry.

Have you ever seen or met someone so breathtakingly attractive that you were moved you in some way to write, sing, paint, sketch, dance? I have met many of such, and, likely, so have you. It is not without reason that God has created humans as the pinnacle of his physical creation- saving the most exquisite for last, maybe?

These next five pieces were written about someone who, in my opinion, is exquisitely good-looking. The way she smiles, her eyes, her lips, and the shape of her face moves me, and is the motivation for the poems you are about to read.

Her physical beauty is moving, earth shattering, and stimulates my imagination. She makes a fine muse.

When I first met her, her eyes and the way her face lit up when she smiled... let me just say that she distracted me from and made me forget whatever it was I was thinking about doing.

She'll probably be reading this, blushing as she does so.

So, if you *are* reading this, missy, enjoy it...

IF

If I were to go blind today, the last thing I would like to see
More than the beauty of the earth, are your eyes staring back at
me.

And should my lips no longer speak, let these be the last words
I say
And the last words from me you hear, you're pleasing, girl, in
many ways.

Your lips- full, so sweet & supple, to stay silent, I'd be remiss
Not to express my craving for the sweetness I long to kiss.

Smooth brown skin, so soft & silky, one of the reasons for this
rhyme,
I'd move earth, stars, moon & heaven to hold your body next to
mine.

Just as in the days of Noah- like water, you flood all my
dreams.
And 'cause you're not in my arms I'm coming apart at the
seams.

A memorable day that summer- the day your beauty had been
born.
A beauty shown, & beauty known by me to be, by you, well
worn.

Oh, the last thing I'd like to see, should my eyes go dark this moment,

Are your eyes staring back at me stirring passions we can foment.

So, now I awaken knowing your body's a land I've not trav'd.

And ever tortured, e'er alone, knowing it's you I'll never have.

MY LAST WORDS

If yours was the last face i'd see

before I close my eyes,

I'd die satisfied

With you as the last to pass my eyes.

If yours were the last lips I'd kiss

Before my days expire,

I would cherish this

'Cause I'd die with passion lit afire.

Your smile will 'ere go with me

Beyond eternity.

This I swear to you;

'Cause your smile brings me to my knees.

The sweet, sweet softness of your skin,

It soothes my wild soul.

I'll remember it

As what warmed me when the nights were cold.

The sensation of loving you-

Let every time we touched

Live in the mem'ry

That I will die loving you so much.

About M

She's broken free from my dreams
To bring sweet pleasure to my life.
She's not quite what she seems
With a sensual innocence to life.

Her eyes are stuff of legend
& her every move is like a dance.
Her beauty's handed down from heaven
and her voice this man enchants.

More About M

She's got curves like Lincoln Drive.
She's THE candy for my eyes.
From every angle, every side
She brings me to my knees.

Her soft voice sets me at ease.
By her touch I'm greatly pleased.
My soul'd be happily appeased
If she were by my side.

To watch her move on the floor;
To dance with one so adored;
Can't be sated, I want much more-
By her I am amazed.

At her beauty she's unfazed.
But I e'er remain in a daze.
Without her I am driven crazed-
Her kiss I'm begging for.

Her name, it moves me to write
About my dreams every nite
Of she and I wrapped oh so tight
In each other's arms.

By her beauty I've been charmed,
And by thoughts of her my heart's warmed.
Her absence would do me great harm.
She makes my dreams take flight.

No Finer Beauty

She was born in August, a most mem'rable day that year.

no equivalent beauty would be born, not for a while.

If you were ever to see her, your eyes would joyfully tear.

Creamy skin, luscious lips, & yes, I'm a slave to her smile.

True, there are many others, but hers is truly unique;

And I must say this, else be remiss- I love how she looks.

My mind is all aclutter. Somewhat my interest is piqued.

Of her poems are writ- enough to fill scores of books.

Enraptured I become each time I look into her eyes,

'cause they speak of a sensual softness that's intriguing.

On a certain day in August, a day not to despise

A girl was born, her beauty, joy to the world is bringing.

As usual, it's normal to praise God for what he's done,
For no finer beauty exists under the sun.

NEVER LET ME FORGET

Before it all ends, before it all comes to nothing,
Before the sun forever sets upon us,
Promise me this, if anything-

That you'll never let me forget that touch that we shared on the
ferris wheel,
when my head began to spin,
and I first began to feel.

Make sure I'll always remember when I held you close and
tight.
The world seemed so small then,
I could reach out and touch the sky.

Knowing then that I had always loved you,
but even still, not knowing why!

Never let me forget, under that hot August sun,
the day our lips met each other, when we became one.
When yours started to tremble, and the wind began to roar.

We shared but a kiss, yet we both wanted more.

Never let me forget my love, that which I swore to you.
Everything I vowed, the promises made,
Everything I said I'd do.

Promise me that you'll be there,
That you'll make me keep in mind all the love I swore to you,
before the beginning of time.

Will you remember me?

Though days have past, and months have come and gone
Though the years have died, and time pushes forward,
  Will you remember me?

Though the sun still shines, and the moon never sleeps
Though the seasons come and go,
  Will you remember me?

As your kiss never left my lips, and your touch my flesh
And my passion for you always plagues my heart
  Oh how I remember you!

Because I tremble when I hear your name,
And I ache to feel your breasts caress me,
I wonder
  Will you remember me the same?

Though our first and last kiss be but a moment
And endless be my thoughts of you,
  Will you remember me too?

Though our paths may ne'er cross again
And our lives take on different meanings,
Though we may ever be in each other's past,
And you haunt my thoughts eternally,
Though we may be separated by time
  I will always remember you.

  Will you remember me?

YOU KISSED ME

I told you it was over,

that I wanted no more...

...Then you touched me.

I told you I never

wanted to see you again...

...Then you hugged me.

I told you my heart

no longer yearned for you...

...And then I looked in your eyes.

I told you that the passion

smoldering deep within me was extinguished...

...Then you kissed me.

When everything was said and done,

when my mind was made up to walk out the door,

when I was just about to close this chapter of my life,

you kissed me.

And, oh! The changes a kiss can make.

Everyone who knows me knows that I have even though I like all manner of women, I have a preference for Latinas. There is a reason for this, but I will not expound upon that here. However, there is this one particular woman who provides the motivation behind these next eight pieces. She knows who she is or, at least, she should.

We met during a time in my life where motivation was hard to come by, and the weight of my world's problems fell hard on my shoulders. Needless to say, she provided a refreshing respite from the thoughts that plagued me then.

The Kind Of Beautiful

She's the kind of beautiful that makes me lose my sleep.

The kind of good-looking that in my memory stinks deep.

Her Hair is soft and long, and she smiles a girlish smile.

I want her out of my head, but just for a little while.

Let my mind soak it all in-

Her soft supple skin

and her legs so thin.

Be she Eastern European or Spanish, I don't know,

either way it doesn't matter, 'cause inside my passion grows.

To see her every week in class is insufficient.

To the power of her beauty I'm helpless, can't resist it

Please- to hold her one more time,

for her to be mine,

for time upon time.

The Storm Inside

There is a storm raging inside of me,

a thirst I cannot quench.

My love for you I can't hide, you see.

My desire for you betrays all of me.

My feelings are deeply entrenched.

There is a war happening no man can know—

The desire I have for you.

The passion for you I can't let show;

my craving for you overwhelms me so,

that I don't know what to do.

Untitled #6

My Dominican, you are the island of my respite, the calming waters of my raging soul. You are the soothing silence of dawn in Philadelphia.

Your body is curved like Lincoln Drive. Your beauty overflows like the Schuykill River after a storm. It is as pleasurable as Boathouse Row at night.

You, Dominican, anger me because you are not yet mine.

Mi dominicana, eres la isla de mi respiro, las aguas calmantes de mi furiosa alma.
Eres el suave silencio del amanecer en Filadelfia.

Tu cuerpo está curvado como Lincoln Drive. Tu belleza se desborda como el Río Schuykill después de una tormenta.
Es tan placentero como Boathouse Row por la noche.

Tú, Dominicana, me enojas porque todavía no eres mía.

Intoxicate My Eyes

Your face, your eyes, your body, your hair…
You ask each day why at you I stare,
and I drink you in with my eyes. My
desire for you I cannot disguise.

If you could see the beauty I see
That has awakened passion in me.
If you could feel exactly what i
Feel when I drink you in with my eyes.

I trip and stumble trying to speak
When seeing your beauty. I get weak
From excitement when you pass me by.
Resisting to look, I dare not try.

My soul, my eyes, intoxicated
By your beauty- inebriated!
This is what happens to me when I
Drink all of your beauty in with my eyes.

ntitled #7

together let us dance, you and I, like lovers long parted.
together, you and i, let us make the earth shake as we make
love.
together let us outshine the sun with the passion of our kisses.
let us, together, stop time as we lay together caressing each
other's nakedness.
but first, my little queen, let us, you and i, exchange vows and
rings
before we do all these other things.

Juntos, bailamos, tú y yo, como amantes separados por mucho
tiempo.
Juntos, tú y yo, hagamos temblar la tierra mientras hacemos el
amor.
juntos vamos a eclipsar el sol con la pasión de nuestros besos.
vamos, juntos, a detener el tiempo mientras nos acostamos
acariciando nuestra desnudez.
pero primero, mi Reina, permítanos, usted y yo, a intercambiar
votos y anillos antes de hacer todo lo demas.

Would that I

Would that I'd for a moment kiss
Your soft, precious, sumptuous lips
I'd give my wealth & fame and decry
The death that awaits a man such as I.

Would that i'd forever embrace
In both my hands your lovely face
I'd waive notoriety then I'd deny
The life belonging to one such as I.

Would that I'd touch skin soft as yours
A body from head to toe that allures,
I'd curse all of heaven to try
The self-control of one such as I.

Ojalá por un momento me besara
Tus labios suaves, preciosos y suntuosos
Daría mi riqueza y fama y condenaré
La muerte que le espera a un hombre como yo

Quisiera acariciar para siempre
En ambas manos tu cara encantadora
Renunciaría a la notoriedad, y negaría
La vida que pertenece a alguien como yo

Ojalá pudiera tocar la piel suave como la tuya
Un cuerpo desde la cabeza a los pies que atrae,
Maldeciría todo el cielo para intentar
El autocontrol de uno como yo.

WITH YOUR HAND IN MINE

Together, my love, with your hand in mine
We'll sail the sea of eternity, traversing time
And for as long as each star stands fixed in the sky
I wish to count them forever, with you by my side.

For you, my love's burning, like an eternal flame
And the wind cooling my body forever whispers your name.

From time immemorial, I've loved only you
And long after time ends, my love'll stand true.

A love, our love, unaffected by time.
I'm yours forever, if you'll only be mine.

CON TU MANO EN LA MÍA

Juntos, mi amor, con tu mano en la mía

Navegaremos el mar de la eternidad, atravesando el tiempo

Y mientras cada estrella permanezca fija en el cielo

Deseo contarlas para siempre, contigo a mi lado

Por ti, mi amor arde, como una llama eterna

Y el viento refresca mi cuerpo para siempre susurra tu nombre

Desde tiempos inmemoriales, solo te he amado

Y mucho después de que termine el tiempo, mi amor se

mantendrá fiel.

Un amor, nuestro amor, no afectado por el tiempo.

Soy tuyo para siempre, si solo eres mía.

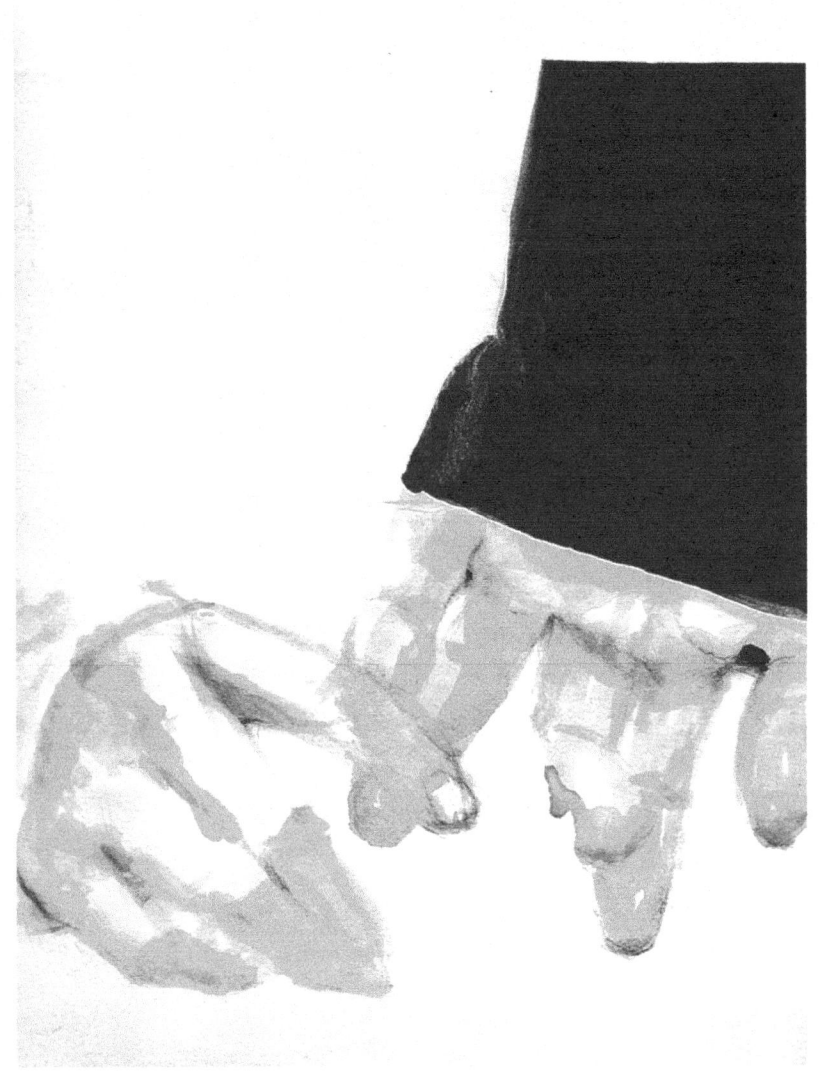

Te quiero conmigo

Te quiero conmigo. No es que tenga nada que decir, solo para poder pasar el día admirando tu belleza.

Te quiero conmigo. Quisiera poder alcanzar tu mano y apretarla junto a la mia.

Te quiero conmigo. Quiero saber que estás sentada a mi lado, aun si todo lo que hacemos es sentarnos en silencio.

Quiero que estés conmigo.

Quiero poder escribir palabras que solo estén motivadas por la pasión que tengo por ti.

Te quiero con migo, para siempre, por siempre.

Te quiero, pequeña hermosa.

Conmigo.

I want you with me. Not that I have anything to say, but just so that I can spend the day admiring your beauty.
I want you with me. I want to be able to just reach out and hold your hand tightly in mine.

I want you with me. I want to be able to know you are sitting next to me, even if all we do is sit in silence.

I want you to be with me.

I want to be able to write words that are only motivated by the passion I have for you.

I want you with me, forever, for always.

I want you, little beautiful girl.

With me.

Untitled #8

You said I'm too old –
and, girl, that was cold,
but it don't change a thing,
I still want you.

And when you are mine
(just give it some time)
I'll kiss every freckle
just to tease you.

I like

I want

I need

I don't want to be without

I want to wake up next to

And go to bed next to

And dream about

I want to think all day about

There's no one I want to be with but

I want to kiss

I want to touch

I want to melt with

I want to dream with

I want to build with

I want a family with

I love

YOU

Somewhere There's a Woman

Somewhere there's a woman

Waiting for my touch.

Somewhere there's a woman

Who'll love me this much.

Somewhere there's a woman

Longin' for my kiss.

Somewhere there's a lady

Whom my lips & body miss.

Somewhere there's a woman

That popped out of my dreams.

Somewhere there's a woman

Who's way of lovin' makes me scream.

She's down wit' me, she'll dance for me

And her lovin' me will set me free.

Someone out there somewhere

Is wanting to love me

Like I want to love her...

Somewhere there's a woman...

Until Then

When the time is right,

    and the mood is sufficient;

When the thunder no longer roars in the sky

    and the winds cease to ravage the land;

Until the sun no longer casts it's golden shadow in the sky

    and the eyes of the universe and over again shine upon

us

      I will tell you I love you.

After I have kissed your lips

    and tasted your sweet passion,

When my blood starts to boil,

    and my skin begins to chill,

When all my thoughts and dreams are of you

    and every face I see is yours,

      then I'll say I love you.

When my body screams out for your touch

    and my lips begin to tremble,

When your scent lingers in my soul

    and the only sound I hear is your voice,

When my heart cries out your name and my lips utter only a

whisper...

    then I will shout to the whole world that
    truly I do love you!

Untitled #9

When I come home from work all is wanna see

Is your soft, sultry eyes staring at me.

The table don't need to be set,

The floor don't need to be swept.

Food fresh from the fire I do not require

I jus' wanna hold you close to me.

Wanting More

I want more than just one lifetime,
more than just this dream.
More than just eternity
more than just to make you mine.

I want more than just your pretty face,
more than just smooth skin;
so much more than just your eyes.
like candy, I want more than just a taste.

More than forever,
us two together,
more than just to kiss
your sweet soft silky lips.
I want more than just one lifetime with you.

RAINFALL

The rain falls
as we look at each other's eyes.
Nothing is said, everything is revealed. Things unheard say
more than the things said.

The rain falls
as I reach out to hold your hand.
Nothing comforts like the touch of a loved one. One touch can
ease a world of pain.

The rain falls
as I take you in my arms.
Until you hold me I do not feel secure. Being held can make all
the difference.

The rain falls
as we kiss. Nothing stirs the soul like the taste of your lips.
Nothing is better said than what is said with a kiss.

The rain falls
when you tell me you love me. Oceans roar, the heavens
rumble. It is said that only one word can move mountains, that
only one word can shape planets, that only one word can mean
so much.

The rain falls.

a stranger

i will always remember your smile.

the smile that could light up a room. the smile that melted away the icicles that were once formed in my heart.

-but now that smile is no more.

i will always remember your eyes.

those beauteous brown eyes that cut deep into my soul, eyes that saw through me, pierced my heart, and pulled me closer to you.

-those eyes no longer see me.

i will always remember your touch.

a touch so soft it shattered the most adamant of shells. a touch so soothing it calmed even the most violent of storms raging inside of me.

-that touch will never again ease me.

i will remember always, our first kiss.

the kiss bringing me to my knees, giving me the strength to move planets, shake galaxies, and like thunder roars in the heavens, let flow the most treasured of words...

no day, no second, no moment will ever be etched in my memory,

embedded in my heart, as the day we shared our first kiss.

-but now that kiss will be as foreign to me as your smile, your eyes, your touch.

your kiss will only be to me but a stranger.

Wandering

Wandering , aimlessly in the darkness,
hoping to find someone who cares.
Reaching out to a heart that's pure;
Only to fine there's no one there.

Praying to God to send me someone to hold;
wishing that one day I'd find someone.
Dreaming of the day I'd wish no more,
only to find another task undone.

Finding someone and falling in love;
man, that's happiness beyond belief!
Ecstasy one day, conflicts the next.
It was conflicts that led to my grief.

Realizing now that I have yet to find
a love that's true and bright,
A love that knows that through all the pain,
we'll have to fight to make it right.

Loneliness, cold, damp, unfeeling;
this, the story of my life.
To know only pain, only misery;
this the sad story of my life.

Untitled #12

i don't know how it feels to cry

i don't know what my tears look like,

> feel like,
> taste like.

i wish i could open the floodgates

> but i lost the key.

do i even know how to cry,

> how to feel?

do i even know the color of my tears?

> no.

do i want to know what they look like?

> what they feel like?

am i cruel, heartless, cold?

don't i care?

i know how it feels to hurt,

i know how pain feels,

but i don't know how to cry, to shed a tear.

Solitude

there are times when i just wanna scream.
why? i don't know.
i just wanna scream.

there are those times i just wanna cry.
why? i don't know
i just wanna.

sometimes i just want to laugh.
why? i don't know.
i just want to.

i don't wanna say anything at all, sometimes.
why? i just don't know.
i just wanna be quiet.

sometimes i just wanna dance.
why? i don't know.
just let me dance.

sometimes i just wanna hit somebody.
why? i don't know.
just get away from me!

sometimes i just don't know myself.
maybe it's just me, i don't know.

The Tears I Cry

The tears I cry are ne'er to be seen. None shall ever see me
bawl.
Literal tears from my eyes don't fall. When I'm hurt my face
stays clean.

The key to within me is perpetually lost, the door is forever
closed.
All things about me no one truly knows, as knowing exacts a
high cost.

Like soldiers of old safe behind walls, like a child in daddy's
strong arms.
My heart is locked up safe from all harm. Ne'er again to
stumble and fall.

About My Wife

her hair, her face, her smile, her curves;

her beauty wreaks havoc on my weathered nerves.

she invades my thoughts when we're apart;

an' just watching her walk- it stops my heart.

torture! Sweet torture. She tortures me!

tear out my eyes so her beauty i can't see!!

Acerca de mi Esposa

su cabello, su rostro, su sonrisa, sus curvas;

su belleza causa tempestad en mis nervios desgastados.

ella invade mis pensamientos cuando estamos aparte;

y solo mirarla caminar- se detiene mi corazón.

¡tortura! Dulce tortura. Ella me tortura!

arranca mis ojos para que su belleza yo no pueda ver!!

YOU!

You own my heart.

You are all I see.

You flood my thoughts.

It is only you that I desire.

TOI!

Vous possédez mon cœur.

Vous êtes tout ce que je vois.

Tu inonde mes pensées.

C'est vous, seulement, que je désire.

Untitled #13

Every curve of your body I long to travel

Ogni curva di tua corpa, io bramare a viaggio

The secrets of your heart, a mystery to unravel

Il segreti di tua cuore, un misterio a dipanare

The taste of your lips to satiate my desire

Il gusto di tua labbra a saziare mio desiderio

Close proximity to you will set me afire.

La vicinanza a te mi farà incendiare.

To Be Your Hero

I wanted to be your Popeye, your Mighty Mouse, your Adam
Ant.

I wanted to save you from all types of badness; then I realized
that I can't.

I wanted to be your hero, the guy you call when you need help.

I wanted to save you from all kinds of hurt. I couldn't save you
from yourself.

I tried to be your Superman- to fly in and save the day.

And i failed to be your Batman. I failed to scare your fears
away.

I'm just a man- no more no less. Get this thing through your
head

I love you, girl, and though it hurts these words must be said

I'm not here to be your hero, not your savior, not your king.

I'm not your knight in shining armor, can't do miraculous
things.

I am and I will always be the man who loves you.

Untitled #14

There was a time a few years back
When I was but a boy
Donned a uniform, learned to fight
Weapons were my toys.

Combat, warfare, blood and guts-
These things I did desire.
But when it comes to love I was not trained;
I'd much rather be under fire.

At least I'd know, with knife in hand
I'd have a fighting chance,
Against a man, maybe two, or three-
But not against romance.

I'd rather take a bullet any day for
The man fightin' 2 my right
Than 2 b uncertain, dazed, confused
By love. Oh! What a blight!

Why didn't it hurt you to hurt me

Why didn't it hurt you to hurt me;
Or did you just not care?
Why'd you choose not to see me
Broken, with my heart laid bare?

Why didn't it hurt you to hurt me?
Did not my tears suffice?
Did it please you to leave me
Empty, while you moved on with life?

What kind of evil monster are you
To tear my heart from my chest?
Is causing pain a game for you?
Is this what you do best?

What kind of fool might I be
To not have seen this first?
Of the two of us I don't see
Which one of us is worse.

You for what you've done, or me for not seeing it.

I wish it on you

Do you know what it's like, comin' home at night to an empty bed?

It messes with your head, and tears your heart apart.

You don't know how it hurts, comin' home from work just to be alone,

Never anyone home; it tears my heart apart.

Did you know that I tried, despite all your lies, faking happiness?

Inside I was a mess. It broke my weary soul.

No one should feel like I feel so deep inside. No one else but you

Should feel what I feel too. You should feel just as cold.

I'm hurt too deeply for apologies.

You lied to my face, made me so disgraced

You played with my mind, and wasted my time

walked out of our home; left me all alone

You have no excuse. Now I say to you

I wouldn't wish this kinda pain on anyone else,

not to feel what I felt when you walked away.

No, I wouldn't wish this pain on no one else...

But I wish it on you.

You've lost me.

I thought we'd share a journey, an adventure all our own.
Out of love I gave my all to you- you left me broken, sad,
alone.

For once I thought I found love, when I gazed into your eyes,
But then I came to realize your charm was none but a disguise.

Now it's my turn to come back, to fight back, to be strong!
You don't get to say you're sorry, to ask me what went wrong,

'Cause if you see me cry
Don't speak to me, After hurting me.
'Cause when you see me cry...

You've lost me.

Untitled #15

When the sky is clear and the storm subsides
Together you and I will fly
as far away as the eye can see
You and me and eternity.

Dear Reader,

Thank you, first of all, for taking the opportunity to consider my poetry. I sincerely hope that you were touched by some, if not all, of it. Mostly, though, I hope it has awakened in you something that motivates you to draw, write, sculpt, sing, whatever. I hope it moves you to action, creative action.

As I compiled the poetry for this, my first book, each one brought back to mind memories that I thought long gone. I hope you, too, had the same experience.

Thanks, again, to reading my poetry.

I hope you enjoyed it.

The author.

SHOUTS OUT-

To **my family**: Mom and Dad; To my Grandma, Lucille; To my sibs (Skip, Michael, Cissi, Kristin, Alan, Katri, Kalyn); my Nieces (Marisa, Jordyn, Tazi, Taylor, Najae); my Nephs (Christopher, Malachi, Julian, Andre, Shion, Lenon, Isaiah, Alexander, Tre); Gwen and Herschel; my in-laws (Traci, Jordan, Kyle, Damaris, Mieko); my heart, Kellie; Stacey; Tanya; my Aunt Arlene (glad to know you're my 'sister', too); my cuzos (Helen, Binga, Tisha, Tina, Robina, Joel, Wendy, Anthony, Hermes [and Mia B.], Kisha, Kirstin, Donna, Aminah, Ant'ney, Quinesha, Quindell, Cynta, Alfred, Anna, Brenda, Geraldine, Dionne, those of my newly found fam [the Baldonasa, Kiamco, and Mondejar families]; Robin, Bernice, and Carla; Bettina, Jarrel, Quindel, Jr.)

Thanks to **my Peeps** (in no specific order): Ashley; Tomekia; M. Bunting; Proc and Mrs. Proc; Mosley; J. Rhodes; C. & G. Younger; V. Freeman; Funchess; Claudette; Don & Zookie; D. & A. Waller; Joi-Joi; Diamond; Dave and Hope; G. Atohun; A. McCann; S. Cavanaugh; Amy; Dob; S. & J. Mapp; Paula; Renee; Linda; April; D. Martin (boot camp was that much more fun); Roenika; E. Lanier; Juanda; Quellory; Angie; Deidra; Sonia, M. & L. Jackson and family.
all my homies from G Btry 3/14; Mr. Vernell Woods and, posthumously, Mr. Cyril Johnson; Robert (Bobby) Kennedy.

Thank you to those who moved me and inspired the poetry that I have written.

Special shouts out to: O. G. Williams, my best friend and fellow troublemaker; L. J. Brown, my best friend and my brother-in-arms; Stevie P.- I will always be proUd of thE man you have become; D. Bellinger, who could make anyone laugh; R. Hooper, my cousin, who I miss.

In memory of Nana Bea, Pop-Pop, Aunt Sara, Aunt Elaine, Nana, Aunt Bessie, and Tammy.

If I have neglected to include someone, please know that you are as important to and loved by me as all who are named herein.